It's Catching

Pinkeye

Angela Royston

Heinemann Library
Chicago, Illinois

Designed by David Oakley/Arnos Design
Illustrations by Jeff Edwards
Originated by Dot Gradations
Printed in Hong Kong, China

06 05 04 03 02
10 9 8 7 6 5 4 3 2

Library of Congress Cataloging-in-Publication Data
Royston, Angela.
      Pink eye / Angela Royston.
          p. ; cm. -- (It's catching)
      Includes bibliographical references and index.
      ISBN 1-58810-230-0
      1. Conjunctivitis--Juvenile literature. [1. Conjunctivitis.]
      [DNLM: 1. Conjunctivitis--Juvenile Literature. WW 312 R892p 2001]
      I. Title. II. Series.

RE230 .R69 2001
617.7'73--dc21
                                        00-012835

Acknowledgments
The Publishers would like to thank the following for permission to reproduce photographs:
Bubbles: pp. 8 Fran Rombout, 14 Ian West, 23 Claire Paxton; pp. 20, 24, 25 Gareth Boden; pp. 10, 22 Martin Soukias; PhotoDisc: pp. 4, 9, 19, 26 Ryan McVay; p. 29 Robert Harding; Science Photo Library: pp. 5, 7, 12 Scott Camazine; 13 Will and Deni McIntyre, 15 John Durham, 16 P. Marazzi, 17 St. Bartholomew's Hospital, 18 Mauro Fermariello, 21 Mark Clarke; Stone: pp. 11 Dennis O'Clair, 28 Robert Daly; p. 27 Peter Cade/Tony Stone.

Cover photograph reproduced with permission of Science Photo Library.

Some words are shown in bold, **like this.** You can find out what they mean by looking in the glossary.

Contents

What Is Pinkeye?

Pinkeye is an **infection** that affects the inside of the eyelid. It can also affect the thin covering of the eye.

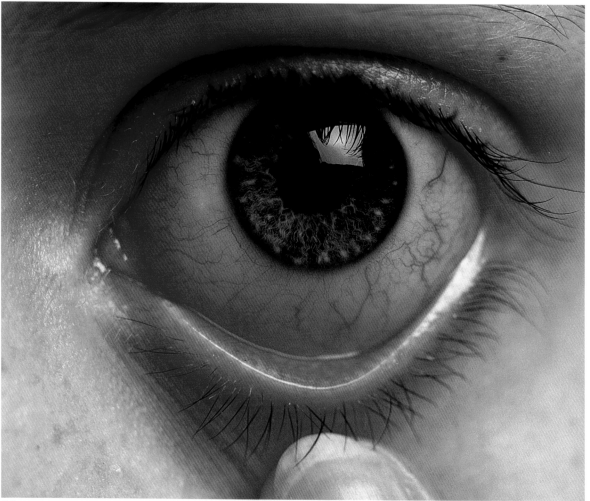

Pinkeye is also called **conjunctivitis.**
Pinkeye is **infectious.** This means it is
passed from one person to another.

Healthy Eyes

You use your eyes to see. Light enters each eye through the **pupil** in the center of the eye.

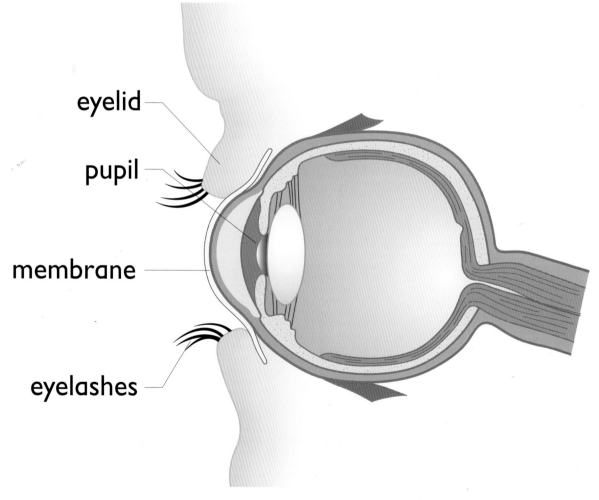

eyelid

pupil

membrane

eyelashes

The eye is covered by a thin skin called a **membrane.** The membrane keeps dirt and **germs** from getting into the eye. So do the eyelids and eyelashes.

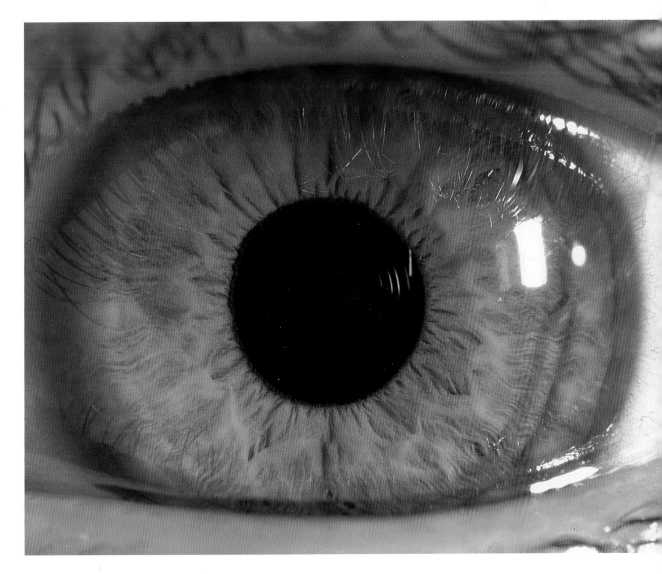

What Causes Pinkeye?

Pinkeye is usually caused by **bacteria** or **viruses.** These **germs** are so tiny that you can only see them through a **microscope.**

This photo shows the virus that causes pinkeye. It has been **magnified** and colored so that you can see it more clearly.

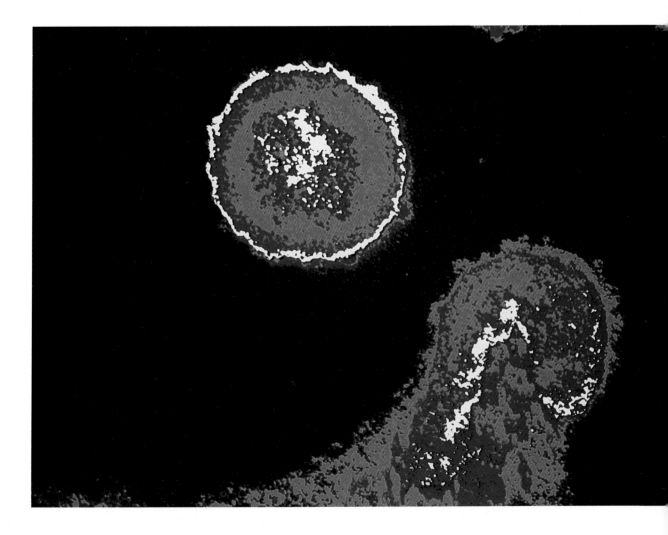

How Do You Catch Pinkeye?

You catch pinkeye when the **bacteria** or **virus** touches your eyes. If a friend has pinkeye, he or she might rub some of the **germs** onto a towel.

If you then use the same towel, you may rub the germs into your own eye. Germs in the swimming pool water may also get into your eyes.

Other Causes

This photo shows tiny grains of **pollen** blown from some grass. Pollen causes **allergies** and itchy, sore eyes. People who suffer from allergies may get pinkeye.

Strong **chemicals** can also cause pinkeye. The chemicals burn the thin covering of the eye. People who use strong chemicals should wear **goggles** to protect their eyes.

First Signs

The first sign of pinkeye is often an itching or burning feeling in the eye. Tears help wash dirt and **germs** out of the eye.

When you have pinkeye, your eye may become a lot more watery than usual. It can also become very red.

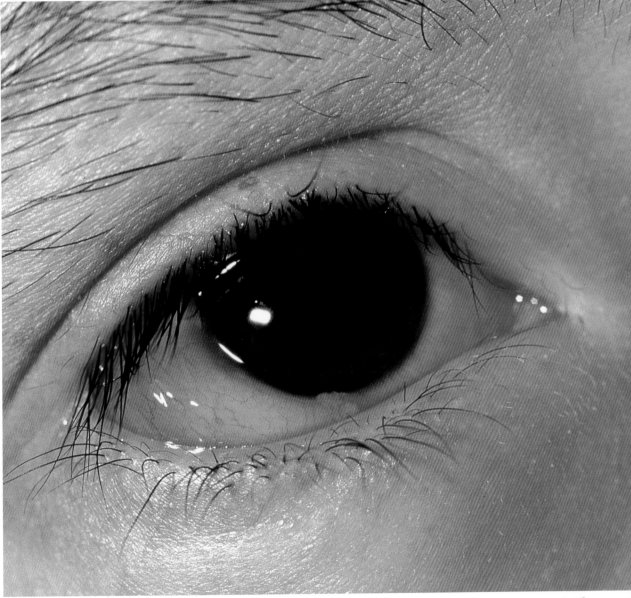

Sticky Eyes

As your body fights the pinkeye **germs,** it makes a sticky, yellow **pus.** When you are asleep, this pus may make your eyelids stick together.

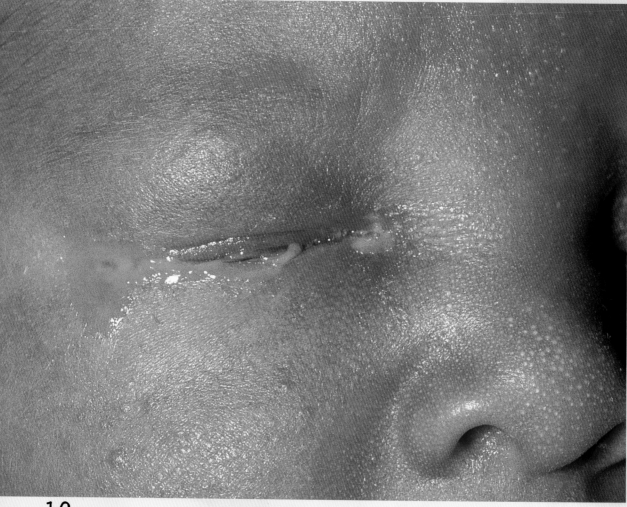

Use a new cotton ball dabbed in clean, fresh water to wipe away the pus. Pinkeye gets its name because the white part of your eye becomes red.

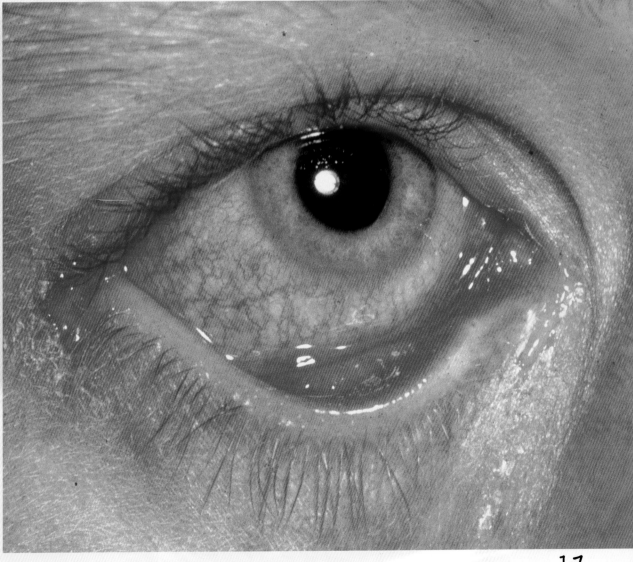

Treatment

If you have pinkeye, you should have it checked by a doctor. If it is caused by a **virus,** you will have to wait for it to get better on its own.

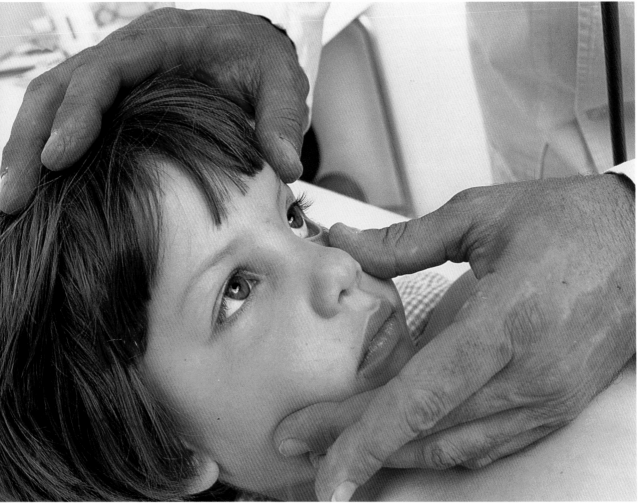

If it is caused by **bacteria,** like the one in this picture, the doctor will give you an **antibiotic ointment.** Antibiotics can kill bacteria. They cannot kill viruses.

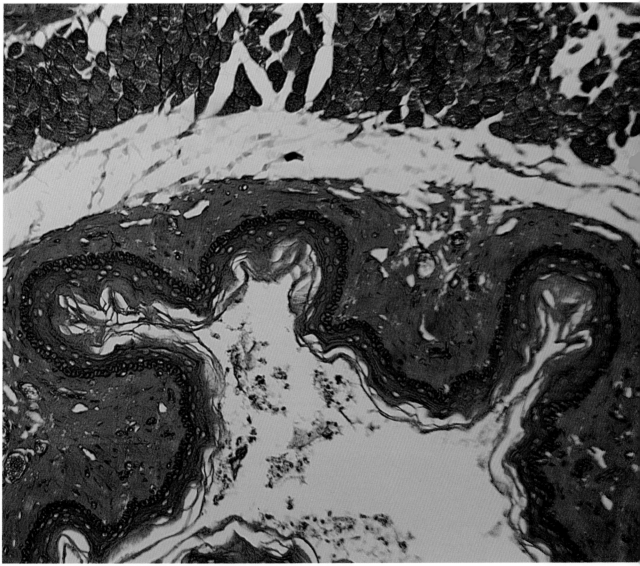

Getting Better

The doctor will tell you how often to apply the **ointment.** An adult may have to squeeze some into your eye for you.

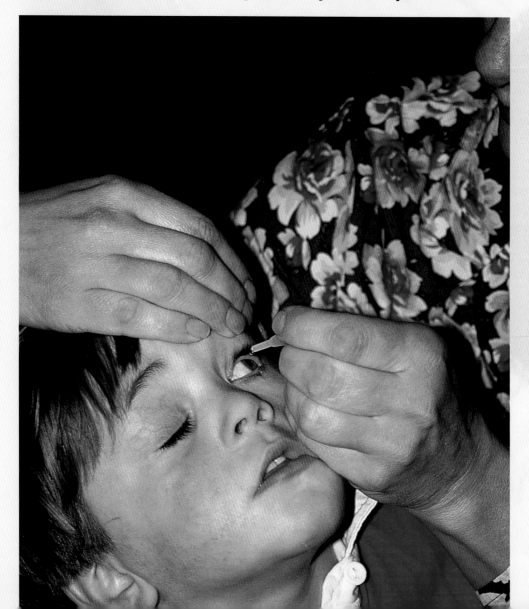

The ointment will start to work after a few days. You must keep using it for as long as the doctor tells you. If you don't, your eye may get sore again.

Other Treatments

If the pinkeye is caused by an **allergy,** a cold **compress** may help. You can make a compress by running cold water over a pad of clean material.

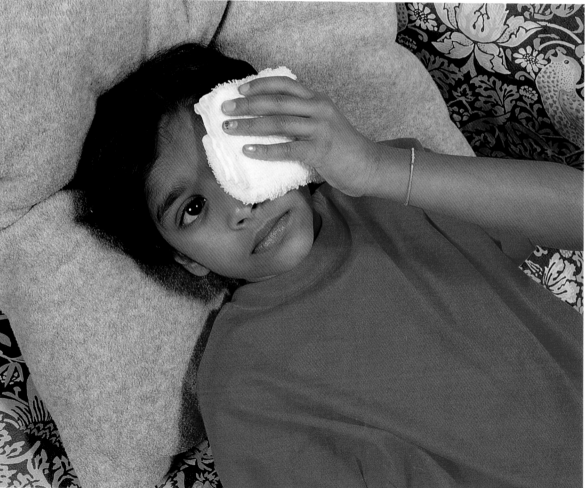

Squeeze out the water and hold the pad over your closed eye. If you get **chemicals** in your eye, bathe it in clean, fresh water. Go see a doctor as soon as you can.

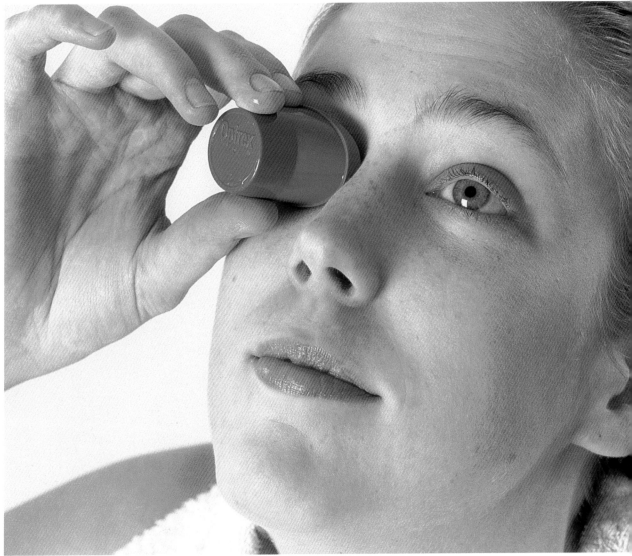

Don't Spread It!

If you have pinkeye or another eye **infection,** try not to pass it on. Don't use towels that other people might use.

Try not to catch pinkeye. Don't rub your eyes with dirty hands. Also, be sure to keep your hair out of your eyes.

Staying Healthy

You are more likely to stay well if you live a healthy life. Get lots of exercise and fresh air.

Eat lots of fresh fruit and raw vegetables.
Wash your face and hands often and get
plenty of sleep.

Think About It!

Sharon has caught pinkeye. She was swimming with her friend in the pool. How might Sharon have caught the eye **infection?***

These children wear swimming **goggles** when they go in the pool. Will goggles keep them from catching pinkeye?*

*Read page 30 to find out.

Answers

Page 28

If her friend has pinkeye, the **germs** could be carried in the water that splashes Sharon's face. The germs could also be on the towel that she uses to dry her face.

Page 29

Swimming **goggles** will help to keep water from splashing in their eyes, but some water may get under the goggles. Pinkeye germs may also be on a towel they use or on their fingers.

Stay Healthy and Safe!

1. Always tell an adult if you feel sick or think there is something wrong with you.

2. Never take any **medicine** or use any **ointment** unless it is given to you by an adult you trust.

3. Remember, the best way to stay healthy and safe is to eat good food, drink lots of water, keep clean, exercise, and get lots of sleep.

Glossary

allergy   something that is harmless to most people but causes a part of the body to become sore or itchy for some people

antibiotic   something that kills bacteria

bacteria   tiny living thing that is usually harmless, but can make you sick if it gets inside your body

chemical   substance that something is made of

compress   pad of material that has been soaked in a soothing liquid

conjunctivitis   another name for pinkeye

germ   tiny living thing that makes you sick if it gets inside your body

goggles   glasses worn to protect the eyes

infection   illness caused by germs

infectious   can be passed from one person to another and can make you sick

magnified   made bigger so that you can see it more clearly

medicine   something used to treat or prevent an illness

membrane   a thin, soft layer of tissue

microscope   something that makes very small things look big enough to see

ointment   oily cream that often contains medicine and is squeezed into the eye or rubbed onto the skin

pollen   powder from flowers and grasses that is blown around by the wind

pupil   the opening in the center of the eye that lets in light

pus   thick liquid made by the body as it fights germs

virus   living thing even smaller than bacteria that can make you sick if it gets inside your body

Index

More Books to Read

Hundley, David H. *Viruses.* Vero Beach, Fla.: Rourke Press, 1998.

Rice, Judith Anne. *Those Ooey Gooey Winky Blinky but . . . Invisible Pinkeye Germs.* Saint Paul, Minn.: Redleaf Press, 2000.

Royston, Angela. *Clean and Healthy.* Chicago: Heinemann Library, 1999.